First World War
and Army of Occupation
War Diary
France, Belgium and Germany

31 DIVISION
94 Infantry Brigade
East Lancashire Regiment
11th Battalion
2 March 1916 - 31 January 1918

WO95/2366/1

The Naval & Military Press Ltd
www.nmarchive.com
Published in association with The National Archives

Published by

The Naval & Military Press Ltd

Unit 10 Ridgewood Industrial Park,

Uckfield, East Sussex,

TN22 5QE England

Tel: +44 (0) 1825 749494

www.naval-military-press.com

www.nmarchive.com

This diary has been reprinted in facsimile from the original. Any imperfections are inevitably reproduced and the quality may fall short of modern type and cartographic standards.

© **Crown Copyright**
Images reproduced by permission of The National Archives, London, England, 2015.

Contents

Document type	Place/Title	Date From	Date To
Heading	WO95/2366-1 11 Battalion East Lancashire Regiment		
Heading	31st Division 94th Infy Bde 11th Bn East Lancs Regt Mar 1916-Jan 1918 To 92 Bde 31 Div		
Miscellaneous	Missing Papers Pro piece reference: WO95/2366 11th Brigade East Lancs Regt. March 1916 to January 1918.	28/10/1991	28/10/1991
War Diary	Huppy	11/03/1916	26/03/1916
War Diary	Longpre	27/03/1916	27/03/1916
War Diary	Vignacourt	28/03/1916	28/03/1916
War Diary	Beaward	29/03/1916	29/03/1916
War Diary	Kantara	02/03/1916	02/03/1916
War Diary	Marseilles	08/03/1916	09/03/1916
War Diary	Bertrancourt	01/04/1916	01/04/1916
War Diary	Courcelles Au Bois	03/04/1916	03/04/1916
War Diary	Colincamps	04/04/1916	30/04/1916
War Diary		01/05/1916	30/05/1916
War Diary	Couecells	01/06/1916	04/06/1916
War Diary	Gozaincourt	05/06/1916	05/06/1916
War Diary	Authine	13/06/1916	13/06/1916
War Diary	Warnimont Wood	14/06/1916	17/06/1916
War Diary	Trenches	19/06/1916	24/06/1916
War Diary	Warnimont Wood	24/06/1916	30/06/1916
Heading	94th Bde.31st Div.WO95/2366 War Diary 11th Battalion East Lancashire Regiment 1st to 31st July 1916		
Heading	War Diary of 11th Bn E. Lancs Rgt 1st July to 31st July 1916		
War Diary	11th East. Lancashire Regt.	01/07/1916	06/07/1916
War Diary	S 30 a 1.5	07/07/1916	31/07/1916
Miscellaneous	Report on Operations June 30th to July 1st Battle of the Somme		
War Diary	Locon	01/08/1916	03/08/1916
War Diary	Trenches	04/08/1916	18/08/1916
War Diary	Locon	18/08/1916	25/08/1916
War Diary	Croix Barbee	26/08/1916	31/08/1916
Heading	War Diary. 11th East Lancs. R. 31st Division September 1916 Vol 7		
War Diary	11 Batt. East Lancashire Regt	01/09/1916	29/09/1916
Heading	War Diary 11th Bn. East Lancs Rgt. 31st Division. October 1916 Volume 55		
War Diary	Festubert	01/10/1916	02/10/1916
War Diary	Village Line Festubert	04/10/1916	04/10/1916
War Diary	Les Choquaux	05/10/1916	05/10/1916
War Diary	Robecq	06/10/1916	06/10/1916
War Diary	Sarton	08/10/1916	18/10/1916
War Diary	Warnimont Wood.	19/10/1916	19/10/1916
War Diary	Trenches	30/10/1916	31/10/1916
Heading	War Diary. 11th Bn. East Lancs Regt 31st Division November 1916 Volume XI Vol 9		
War Diary	Trenches Dell	01/11/1916	03/11/1916
War Diary	Coigneux & Couitcelles.	07/11/1916	07/11/1916

War Diary	Watnimont Wood. & Courcelles.	10/11/1916	10/11/1916
War Diary		11/11/1916	12/11/1916
War Diary	Trenches	14/11/1916	14/11/1916
War Diary	Shilly au Bois	18/11/1916	18/11/1916
War Diary	Trenches	22/11/1916	25/11/1916
War Diary	Shilly au Bois.	28/11/1916	30/11/1916
Heading	War Diary. 11th Bn East Lancs. Regt. 31st Division December 1916 Volume 48 Vol 10		
War Diary	Sailly-au-Bois	01/12/1916	02/12/1916
War Diary	Trenches (Hebuterne)	03/12/1916	03/12/1916
War Diary	Sailly-au-Bois	07/12/1916	09/12/1916
War Diary	Trenches (Hebuterne)	12/12/1916	13/12/1916
War Diary	Rossignol Farm (Coigneux)	17/12/1916	24/12/1916
War Diary	Sailly-au-Bois	25/12/1916	25/12/1916
War Diary	Trenches (Hebuterne)	29/12/1916	29/12/1916
Miscellaneous Heading	War Diary 11th Bn East Lancs Regt. 31st Division January 1917 Volume VIII Vol XI		
War Diary	Trenches Hebuterne	02/01/1917	02/01/1917
War Diary	Sailly-au-Bois Dell	05/01/1917	05/01/1917
War Diary	Beauval.	11/01/1917	19/01/1917
War Diary	Fienvillers.	22/01/1917	26/01/1917
War Diary	Fieffes	29/01/1917	29/01/1917
Heading	War Diary. 11th Battalion East Lancs. Regt. 31st Division February 1917 Volume XIV. 42		
War Diary	Fieffes.	15/02/1917	17/02/1917
War Diary	Terramesnil	20/02/1917	20/02/1917
War Diary	Coigneux	21/02/1917	26/02/1917
Heading	War Diary. 11th Bn. East Lancs Regt. 31st Division March 1917 Volume XV Vol 13		
War Diary	Coigneux	01/03/1917	24/03/1917
War Diary	Merville	25/03/1917	31/03/1917
Heading	War Diary. 11th Bn. East Lancs Regt. 31st Division April 1917 Volume XVI Vol 14		
War Diary	Merville	01/04/1917	08/04/1917
War Diary	Fovquereuil	08/04/1917	11/04/1917
War Diary	Houchin	11/04/1917	11/04/1917
War Diary	Magnicourt-En-Commte	14/04/1917	14/04/1917
War Diary	Ecoivres	29/04/1917	29/04/1917
War Diary	Maroeuil.	30/04/1917	30/04/1917
Heading	War Diary 11th Bn East Lancs. R. 31st Division May 1917 Volume XVII Vol 15		
War Diary	Maroeuil.	01/05/1917	01/05/1917
War Diary	Roclincourt	02/05/1917	02/05/1917
War Diary	Front Line Oppy Subsection	03/05/1917	03/05/1917
War Diary	Bailleul	04/05/1917	04/05/1917
War Diary	Bois de La Maison Blanche	05/05/1917	05/05/1917
War Diary	Front Line Oppy	07/05/1917	09/05/1917
War Diary	Railway Cutting Bailleul	10/05/1917	10/05/1917
War Diary	Front Line	12/05/1917	31/05/1917
Heading	War Diary. 11th Bn. East Lancs. Regt. 31st Division June 1917 Volume XVII Vol 16		
War Diary	Roclincourt	01/06/1917	30/06/1917
Miscellaneous Heading	War Diary. 11th Bn East Lancashire Regt. 31st Division July 1917. Volume XIX Vol 17		

War Diary			01/07/1917	29/07/1917
Heading	War Diary. 11th Bn. East Lancs Regt. 94-31st Division August 1917 Volume XX Vol 18			
War Diary	Front Line Acheville S		01/08/1917	04/08/1917
War Diary	Thelus		05/08/1917	10/08/1917
War Diary	Front Line		10/08/1917	16/08/1917
War Diary	Mont St Eloy		19/08/1917	24/08/1917
War Diary	Brigade Spt.		25/08/1917	29/08/1917
War Diary	Front Line		29/08/1917	31/08/1917
War Diary				
Heading	War Diary. 11th Bn. East Lanc Regt 31st Division September 1917 Volume XXI Vol 19			
War Diary	Front Line Acheville		04/09/1917	05/09/1917
War Diary	Thelus		05/09/1917	05/09/1917
War Diary	Ecurie		07/09/1917	07/09/1917
War Diary	Farbus.		11/09/1917	18/09/1917
War Diary	Willerval		18/09/1917	24/09/1917
War Diary	Front Line. Acheville.		24/09/1917	24/09/1917
War Diary	Ecurie		25/09/1917	25/09/1917
Heading	War Diary 11th Battn East Lanc R. 31st Division October 1917 Volume XXII Vol 20			
War Diary	Springvale Camp		01/10/1917	01/10/1917
War Diary	Brown Line		06/10/1917	06/10/1917
War Diary	Red Line		12/10/1917	16/10/1917
War Diary	Front Line Acheville		18/10/1917	30/10/1917
Heading	War Diary 11th Battn East Lanc. Regt. 31st Division November 1917 Volume XXIII Vol 21			
War Diary	Front Line Sppy Sector		21/11/1917	21/11/1917
War Diary	Ecurie		27/11/1917	30/11/1917
War Diary	Brion Line Farbus.		01/11/1917	05/11/1917
War Diary	Red Line		05/11/1917	05/11/1917
War Diary	Front Line Acheville		11/11/1917	13/11/1917
War Diary	Ecurie		17/11/1917	17/11/1917
War Diary	Bois de La Maison Blanche		20/11/1917	20/11/1917
Heading	War Diary. 11th Battn. East Lanc. Regt. 31st Division December 1917. Volume XXIII Vol 22			
War Diary	Ewrie		01/12/1917	03/12/1917
War Diary	Oppy		03/12/1917	07/12/1917
War Diary	Egivres		07/12/1917	20/12/1917
War Diary	Neuville St Vaast		20/12/1917	31/12/1917
War Diary				
Heading	94th Brigade 31st Division. 1/11th Battalion East Lancashire Regiment January 1918			
War Diary	Ecurie		01/01/1918	05/01/1918
War Diary	Hudson Post		06/01/1918	12/01/1918
War Diary	Cubitt Camp. (Neuville St. Vaast)		12/01/1918	18/01/1918
War Diary	Vancouver Rd.		18/01/1918	24/01/1918
War Diary	Ecurie		24/01/1918	30/01/1918
War Diary	Houson Post		30/01/1918	31/01/1918
War Diary	Eourie		01/01/1918	05/01/1918
War Diary	Hudson Post.		06/01/1918	12/01/1918
War Diary	Cubitt Camp. (Neuville St. Vaast)		12/01/1918	18/01/1918
War Diary	Vancouver Road.		18/01/1918	24/01/1918
War Diary	Ecurie		24/01/1918	30/01/1918
War Diary	Hudson Post.		30/01/1918	31/01/1918

WO/95/2366

1/1 11 Battalion East Lancashire Regiment.

31ST DIVISION
94TH INFY BDE

11TH BN EAST LANCS REGT
MAR
~~APR~~ 1916 - JAN 1918

To 92 BDE 31 DIV

MISSING PAPERS

PRO piece reference: W.O. 95 / 2366. 11th Brigade East Lancs Regt.
March 1916 to January 1918.

Papers from records in this class and six other classes of public records relating to air operations in the Wars of 1914-1918 and 1939-1945 (AIR 1, AIR 4, AIR 27, AIR 28, AIR 50, ADM 207 and WO 95) were discovered in 1989 and 1990 to be missing. Investigations led to the conviction of a PRO reader on charges of theft and criminal damage; and many of the papers were subseqeuntly recovered.

The following papers from this piece were recovered and returned to their proper places:

    Folio or page numbers:

        ff. 22 - 28.

Where it has not been possible to restore papers to their proper places with certainly the papers recovered have been placed at the end of the piece and given the following folio or page numbers:

Further papers may still be missing from this piece.

Signed: E. O'Deel

Date: 28 October 1991.

MGT 39.1

Army Form C. 2118.

WAR DIARY
or
INTELLIGENCE SUMMARY.

(Erase heading not required.)

Instructions regarding War Diaries and Intelligence Summaries are contained in F.S. Regs., Part II. and the Staff Manual respectively. Title pages will be prepared in manuscript.

Place	Date	Hour	Summary of Events and Information	Remarks and references to Appendices
Hupy	11/3/16	12 A.M.	Arrive at Pont Remy Station and march to Huppy where the Battn is billeted.	A.8.
	16/3/16	8 P.M.	16 Company leave in buses and proceed to Gezaincourt. 2 N.Co. & 20 y Coy. to Rosalles.	a.f
Huppy	26/3/16	8 A.M.	Battalion (less & Coy) marches to Longpre and is billeted.	a.f
Longpre	27/3/16	8 A.M.	Battalion less & Company marches to Vignacourt and is billeted	a.f
Vignacourt	28/3/16	8 A.M.	Battalion less & Company marches to Beauval and is billeted	a.f
Beauval	29/3/16	8 P.M.	Battalion less & Company marches to Bertrancourt and is billeted.	a.f

A.Sells
Capt & Adjt
11 Sbn East Lancs Regt

11th E. LANCS. PART OF VOL. I.

31st DIVn

WAR DIARY (Rest under M.E.F.7)
or
INTELLIGENCE SUMMARY.

Army Form C. 2118.

Place	Date	Hour	Summary of Events and Information	Remarks and references to Appendices
RANTRA	2/3/16		Battalion proceeds to Portland and entrains en route Marseilles Cuella. 2/Lt Nelson & 67 O.R. remain at Port Said	AB
Marseilles	6/3/16			AB
	7/3/16	7 AM	The Battalion arrives at Marseilles and remains on board Ivernia/Ivernich, and entrain for North France.	AB

A Kellogg
Col (A/W)
11th S.Bn East Lancs Rgt.

1.Z
2 sheets

WAR DIARY
or
INTELLIGENCE SUMMARY.
(Erase heading not required.)

Army Form C. 2118.

11 East Lancs
Vol 2

Place	Date	Hour	Summary of Events and Information	Remarks and references to Appendices
BERTRANCOURT	1-4-16	9.30 P.M.	94th INF. BDE Operation Order No 22 received. Ref Map FRANCE Sheet 57D Scale ¼0000. 1.— The 11th EAST LANCS. REGT will move on the 3rd April 1916 to COURCELLES au BOIS, taking over billets from the 14th YORK and LANCS REGT. It will leave the starting point, road junction J 33 d 67 at 3 P.M. On arrival at COURCELLES au BOIS, the Battalion will come under the orders of the G.O.C. 144th F. Infantry Brigade. 2.— The Lewis Gun Detachment of the 11th EAST LANCS REGT will, on the 3rd April 1916 at a time to be arranged by the BDE. M.G. officer take over four gun emplacements now occupied by the M.G. Company of the 144th BDE.	ad ad
COURCELLES au BOIS	3-4-16	3 P.M.	Battalion moved to COURCELLES au BOIS	
COURCELLES au BOIS	3-4-16	7 P.M.	Order received from 144 INF.BDE. addressed O.C. 11th EAST LANCS 'You will move tomorrow to COLINCAMPS — Hour of start 11 A.M — You will move in ½ Platoons, 200 yds interval between each party'.	ad
COLINCAMPS	4-4-16	11 A.M	Battalion moved into BOLINCAMPS and is billeted. Battn is in BDE. Reserve Transport remains at COURCELLES au BOIS	ad
COLINCAMPS	6-4-16	9.45 P.M	Orders given verbally by G.O.C. 94th INF BDE to man known trenches, in consequence of artillery activity on our own and enemy's side	ad

Army Form C. 2118.

WAR DIARY
or
INTELLIGENCE SUMMARY.

(Erase heading not required.)

11th S.B. East Lancs Regt

Place	Date	Hour	Summary of Events and Information	Remarks and references to Appendices
	6.4.16	11:15 pm	Signal message to return to Billets and stand by.	a.s.
	12.4.16		Battn. move to Bertrancourt to Divisional Reserve	a.s.
	23.4.16		Lieut. Lucas started home 2nd Class for a course.	
	28.4.16		Battn. took over front line trenches. Reference maps FRANCE 57D NE 3 & 4 (part of) and 57D SE 1 & 2 (parts of) The disposition were three companies in front line, one company in Reserve. Battn. frontage O+d 45 to K35a 3570. Z Coy on the left Y Company Centre and W Coy right. For the first four days a Coy of the 12th York & Lanc Rgt was were Company, and a Coy of the 14th York & Lanc. for the second four days. 1 man wounded.	
	29.4.16	11:30 pm	A bombardment started on the right of the Battn. line for a raid made by the 29th D.[Division] men who were on the right. The Battn. shot 16. Killed 1. 30.4.16 1:20 am 30.4.16. Casualties 1 killed 1 died of wounds (in hospital) 7 wounded	a.s.
	30.4.16.		Casualties 1 killed 1 wounded.	a.s.

A.W. Smith
Capt & Adjutant

Army Form C. 2118.

WAR DIARY
or
INTELLIGENCE SUMMARY.
(Erase heading not required.)

11th EAST LANCS   Vol 3

Place	Date	Hour	Summary of Events and Information	Remarks and references to Appendices
COURCELLES	1-5-16		During the 5 days occupation of the trenches, wire communicating trenches general up. Saps improved for advanced listening posts, and in our front wiring from K.35.a.30.45" to K.35.a.60.90 in front of the wire recaptured. Was improved with the idea of making it the front line trench. The southern half of this trench was in the Battn. area.	c.7
	4-5-16		One man wounded.	A.8
	5-5-16		One man wounded.	A.9 Ag
			Total Casualties during tour of duty:- 2 killed; one died of wounds; twelve wounded; two slightly wounded who remained at duty.	
	6-5-16		Battn. relieved by the 13th East Yorks and goes into Divisional reserve at Bois du WARNIMONT (in huts.)	A.P.
	15-5-16		The Battn. move to COURCELLES at short notice.	A.P.
	20-5-16		The Battn. went into the front line and recaptured	c.7 2 sheets

Army Form C. 2118.

WAR DIARY
INTELLIGENCE SUMMARY.
(Erase heading not required.)

11TH EAST LANCS REGT

Place	Date	Hour	Summary of Events and Information	Remarks and references to Appendices
	26-5-16		from K 29 c 8595 to K 23 d 2555 (Mat. 57D NE Part 3 & 4) the 8R Worcester being on the right flank and the 12 KO Yorks on the right. In the first five days there were no casualties. All available men were working on improvement of the front line trench, and wiring parties were out every night.	AS
	27-5-16		78 OR transferred from the Cyclists to the Battalion, and joined still the Battalion was in the trenches. 2 men killed. 8 men wounded.	AS
	27-5-16		Lieut Berry-Street of the strength of the Battn, on being granted 3 months leave by the War Office, ceases to be Bomb Offr.	AS AS
	29-5-16		5 men wounded.	AS
			Total casualties during this Tour in the Trenches killed 2, wounded 23.	
	30-5-16		Battn relieved by 14th York & Lancs, and came out to Brigade Reserve in Courcelles.	AP

CEArlingshaw
Lt Col

Army Form C. 2118.

WAR DIARY
or
INTELLIGENCE SUMMARY.

(Erase heading not required.)

June
11 East Lancs
Vol 4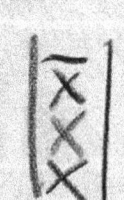
XXXI

A.Z.
2 sheets

Place	Date	Hour	Summary of Events and Information	Remarks and references to Appendices
Couturelles	1/6/16 to 4/6/16		Battalion in Brigade reserve, providing working parties for Brigade.	
Gezaincourt	5/6/16		March from COUTURELLES to WARNIMONT WOOD. RUTTLE and remained there until the 13th. During this period the Brigade carried out special training for the forthcoming attack at RUTTLE being inspected by the Corps Commander and a Brigade of RUTTLE being inspected by the Corps Commander consisted in the attack.	
Authie	13/6/16		Proceeded to camp in WARNIMONT WOOD, remainder marched	
Warnimont Wood	14/6/16 to 18/6/16		19/6/16. This period was spent in completing arrangements for the attack and providing working parties in the trenches.	
	17/6/16		Lts. HITCHEN, GAY, WILLIAMS and 2/Lt. LETT reported for duty.	
Trenches	19/6/16		Proceeded to the trenches taking over the line from the 12th YORK & LANCS REGT and relieving from WARLEY ST to WARNE ST in the CO. IN CAMPS sector. Casualties for this tour in the trenches 12 R.W.S as 24 wounds.	
	23/24		Relieved by the 10th E. YORKS REGT and marched back to	

Army Form C. 2118.

WAR DIARY
or
INTELLIGENCE SUMMARY.
(Erase heading not required.)

Instructions regarding War Diaries and Intelligence Summaries are contained in F. S. Regs., Part II. and the Staff Manual respectively. Title pages will be prepared in manuscript.

Place	Date	Hour	Summary of Events and Information	Remarks and references to Appendices
WARNIMONT WOOD	24/6/16		WARNIMONT WOOD 2nd Lt RITCHIE and 55 men reports for duty. Parties at WARNIMONT WOOD spent in further preparation for the attack.	66
	30/6/16	6.45 p.m	Marched via COURCELLES (4 points) and arrived in position 4 am. 1/7/16	

J.G. Macalpin
Lt + Adjt. 1/8 Argyle Regt.

1577 Wt. W10791/1773 500,000 5/15 D. D. & L. A.D.S.S./Forms/C. 2118.

94th Bde.
31st Div.

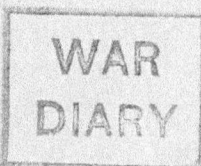

WAR DIARY

11th BATTALION

EAST LANCASHIRE REGIMENT

1st to 31st JULY 1916

Attached = Report on Operations 1st July 1916.

Confidential   Vol 5

G4/31

War Diary

of

11th Bn. E. Lancs. Regt.

1st July to 31st July 1916

5.
6 sheets

WAR DIARY
INTELLIGENCE SUMMARY

Army Form C. 2118.

Place	Date	Hour	Summary of Events and Information	Remarks and references to Appendices
11" EAST LANCASHIRE REGT.	July 1916. 1st		The assembly trenches for the attack extended from MARK COPSE to MATTHEW & COPSE whence up to BASIN YORK in Lancashire Rept on the left and the 93rd Brigade on the right the 12" and 14" Batt" York and Lancaster Regt. were in support to the 11" E. Lancr. Regt + 12" York + Lancr. Regt. The Battalion was ordered to go forward accompanied by detach. from 1" 94" Machine Gun Company and 12" Batt" K.O.Y.L.I. (Pioneers), the hour to attack being 7.30 am. The Regt rapidly advanced heavy rifle and machine gun fire was opened from in front and enfilade fire to attack is of the POINT and GOMMECOURT WOOD. A heavy artillery barrage was also placed on our front line trenches from which though heavy casualties appeared to only a few machine gun enemy from time to time stopped much of my to be of the movement of the forward line	

WAR DIARY or INTELLIGENCE SUMMARY

Army Form C. 2118.

Place	Date	Hour	Summary of Events and Information	Remarks and references to Appendices
	2nd	1am	Small parties penetrated as far as the German front line, but were met with rifle fire. During the day the wounded were returning and had to remain in the shell holes until they returned in the front line night & am on 15th	
	3rd July		When wounded by the attack. Both Herr were situated on flanks & Sap C (T 29 a 93 my map). Lance Corporal Trigg (10th Lanc) & Lieut of Sap Coy called with Germans to surrender 13 Officers including the Commanding Officer & were taken prisoner. Casualties: wounds 76 including 35 wounded & 140. On 4th July the battalion was relieved to POLAND FRENCH. (45 hours) when we were at 14 Officers + 60 other ranks. Thence we occupied huts the night at 4 1/2. July when relieved by a company of the 6 Gloucester Regt. Then both proceeded by night to LOVENCOURT. Marched to LOVENCOURT to GEZAINCOURT, marching to Brigade	

S/v

Army Form C.2118.

WAR DIARY
or
INTELLIGENCE SUMMARY.
(Erase heading not required.)

Place	Date	Hour	Summary of Events and Information	Remarks and references to Appendices
Sara	15	7⁰ᵅ a.m.	was at one time truent PONT DE NIEPPE, but that they were later counter-attacked and forced to withdraw to the NIEPPE SYSTEM. The line therefore remained practically unchanged. There is now no doubt that the enemy intends to hold the line he has now to its same strength, and it appears that more thorough measures will have to be taken to dislodge him.	
		8⁴	The 92ⁿᵈ Infy. Bde on the right started an attack at 5.30 a.m. The plan App. 056 was for two Companies to form up on the inter Bde boundary South of ROMERSTRAAT and to attack Southwards, clearing the area up to the PLOEGSTEERT - LE BIZET road	

WAR DIARY
or
INTELLIGENCE SUMMARY.
(Erase heading not required.)

Army Form C. 2118.

Instructions regarding War Diaries and Intelligence Summaries are contained in F. S. Regs., Part II. and the Staff Manual respectively. Title pages will be prepared in manuscript.

Place	Date	Hour	Summary of Events and Information	Remarks and references to Appendices
	8-		March S. from GÉZAINCOURT to FRÉVENT and entrained there for STEENBECQUE when arrived at 9.30 pm. Bivouacked for night in the Forêt du NIEPPE and marched to CALONNE sur LYS	
	9-		During the march the battalion was at Calonne, was sent on reconnaissance.	
	15-		Passed by march route to billets at Gonnehem, Rue du PUITS, when battalion was in Brigade reserve	
	16- 20-		Draft of 12 Officers arrived Draft of 3 Officers arrived. During the period 16-20th every possible step was taken to trades and training in Lewis Gun + Bombing was carried on	
	24-		A composite company of 6 Officers and 160 O Ranks under Capt. Kershaw was detailed to X-2 Company was attached to the 13th York — handed to report for duty to	

1577 Wt. W10791/1773 500,000 1/15 D. D. & L. A.D.S.S./Forms/C. 2118.

Army Form C. 2118.

WAR DIARY
or
INTELLIGENCE SUMMARY.

(Erase heading not required.)

Place	Date	Hour	Summary of Events and Information	Remarks and references to Appendices
	27—		Truchan. 15—x Companies left the setting point St VAAST, TRAG 3, BONES, SPITTO d'ANGLE. Battalion was due on billets in LECONTURE to LESPIEM when Regimen was signed by the composite company and became concentrated there.	
	27—31		Draft ji Stres and Training of Bombers & Lewis Gunners continued and route marching	

R. Newton
Command 11th B.O. East Lancs Regt.

Report on operations June 30th to
9.40 PM July 1st - Battle of the Somme

7 PM.
30·VI-16

7 pm
30.6.16

The 11th East Lancashire Regt marched off according to Time Table along the prescribed Route at 7 PM 30·VI·16 and reached

8.30 PM

8.30 pm

Courcelles at 8.30 PM where tea was served to the men.

9/40 PM

9/20 pm

After synchronising watches at 9.30 PM the head of the Column left Courcelles 9·45 PM and marched as directed to Central Avenue. The trench was in a very bad state and over the knee deep in mud which had become glutinous. As the fork in Central Avenue

12.20 am
1/7/16

12.20 am
1·7·16

had not been reached by 12.20 am — I proceeded to the head of the 2nd wave and ordered them to go overland. I reported this to 94th Brigade at entrance to Central Avenue.

After coming to the batteries the Regiment had proceeded in the Trench way to the batteries firing. I reached with the head of the Column the front line system of trenches at 2.20 am — Where I found that orders had been issued by higher command that Sap D & Sap C were not to be occupied by any troops. Accordingly that it made

Fresh Dispositions for the accommodation of my first wave – I accommodated No 1 & 11 Platoon W Company between Warley Avenue and 29 A 93 No 5 & 6 Platoon X Company between this point & Board Copse inclusive in the positions from which the 1st wave would start. They were accommodated in partially blown in fire bays & Duffle Trench. The wave being under command of Capt Tayl[or]
The 2nd Wave was under command of Capt Livesey and was accommodated in Copse Trench –
The 3rd Wave under 2/Lt Williams in Campion.
4th Wave in Monk 12. under Capt Riley
Head Quarters at Mouth of Sap C –
During the night & early morning there was a constant bombardment. Attention was paid to Rob Roy and the Front Line.

7.20 a.m.   At 7.20 a.m. the hurricane bombardment 7.20.am opened and the first wave crossed into No Mans Land – The Germans opened almost immediately with M.G. & Rifle fire putting on a few minutes later an intense barrage –

7.22 a / 7.22 am   The 2nd wave proceeded to follow the 1st
                   wave onto No Mans Land
7.23 a / 7.23 am   Our platoon 13 & 5 crossed following my 2nd wave
7.29   / 7.29 am   I saw my 3rd & 4th waves advancing from
                   Campion & Brock Respectively
                   By this time there was intense Rifle M.G.
                   Fire and a very heavy barrage of artillery
                   Fire
                   They crossed into No Mans Land crossing
                   the front line about 7.32 am
7.39   / 7.39 am   Reported by runner via Mash Copse 1st line.
                   Waves advanced according to time Table
                   Heavy M.G. & Rifle Fire still coming from German
                   1st line. Intense Fire of all descriptions
7.42 a / 7.42 am   Reported by runner Intense fire of all descriptions
7.50 a / 7.50 am   Reported by runner all four waves have gone
                   forward. – M.G. Fire still coming from the North
                   Report from Lt GAY. Self Platoon through
                   1st Line Lt Gay wounded
                   M.G. Fire much less intense –
                   I sent Lt MacAlpine to establish telephone
                   communication between Mash Copse & my
                   H.Q. Lt MacAlpine returned & informed
                   me all communication was cut & it was
                   not reestablished all day

8.10 a.m & 8.10 am — I reported M.G. fire still coming from the North traversing from beyond Mark Copse over Sap C.

Capt Guerny 13th Y & L arrived with only 9 men in his two platoons.

I further Reported I could see odd groups in my front believed to be wounded

Also that I could not see any of my waves

No further Report from waves

Heavy Artillery Barrage on front line

8.22 & 8.22 am — Machine Gun fire still coming from direction of Mark Copse
Heavy Artillery Barrage Front Line
No information from my waves

R.J. Line not entered about 8.35.
Very little Rifle Fire to my front. Heavy M.G. fire still coming from my left over Mark Copse. And now & then a burst from Right
No information from my waves

9 a.m & 9 am — Report from Corpl Rigby wounded. belongs to 1st Wave States that only 7 of his platoon got into 1st Line

They held it for about 20 minutes. Bombing
Germans back till Bombs were exhausted
Capt Livesay was with Corp¹ Pugh & was
Wounded

Corp¹ Pugh saw remains of 2ⁿᵈ wave in
front of our barbed wire

Germans still holding out
    Saw no sign of 3ʳᵈ or 4ᵗʰ wave
    Heavy Barrage on front line
    Capt Curran 13Y&L reported arrival
    Capt Smith 13Y&L was informed was going
forward to 2ⁿᵈ line German trenches

10.19.40.1. am No Report from my waves. Germans heavily
    shelled. Capt Roberts RAMC wounded
    Message from OC 13Y&L that C Company
    13Y&L (Capt Curran) was going forward to
    occupy German 1ˢᵗ Line Trenches
    Heavy Barrage front line Trenches MG fire
    from Right.

    Capt Curran is putting his Company in
    front line from Machine Gun & dug C

10 wounded men. 11ᵗʰ E.L. have
returned a Hy. & tale Front line still
in German hands.

~~Lt Ryder seriously wounded 2ⁿᵈ line~~

11.25 (11hr25am) No information from my runners

3ᵗʰ flmer [1ˢᵗ wave] Asiman Capt Livesey states
1ˢᵗ wave encountered heavy M.G. Rifle &
Grenades & Bombs & Artillery fire in
crossing No Mans Land.

Capt Livesey 1ˢᵗ wave with remnants of 2ⁿᵈ
  wave. together with 3ʳᵈ wave charged
  German trenches led by Capt Livesey
  Lt Thompson also entered German trenches
  Lt Ashwell wounded

Between 1ˢᵗ & 2ⁿᵈ line German trenches
Capt Livesey sent back a message for
reinforcement — this never reached me —

Capt Curran is holding from Mullen Copse
de Sap C. 18ᵗʰ W. Yorks prolong his line to
the South

A number of wounded in Sap C & in
  Reserve. Field Dressings urgently required

11.50 11.22 pm Capt & Adjt Peltzer & Lt Ryden wounded.
                Lt Ryden remained on duty.
                No Reports from my Coys except Statement
                of wounded men
                Asked for reinforcement of one Company as only
                a few of Capt Curran's party arrived
                Was promised Company HXQ - They never arrived

12 noon 12 noon I proceeded to put Front Line in
                state of defence as far as possible agst
                Counterattack - Sap C. which had been
                opened up - was blocked by bomb stops
                Asked Staff Capt for supply of Bombs
                Which arrived later

3.10 3.10 pm   The General Western 72nd Brigade
                occupying Sap C were withdrawn
                and put in emplacements on
                right & left of Sap C. I went along my
                whole front line and reported there were
                very few troops defensible - Men nearly
                drawn out of them and cross the Don
                Ezoena. 93rd Brigade have withdrawn
                their men and I have only left 1 off & 25 O.R.

of my own Regiment available 2 Stokes Guns
in position and details of 110421 & Capt
Curran & Capt Gurney and about 30 men — 13 Y.L.
12d Y.L. &c. & are in Mart Copse &
have no one except their H.Q. and that
they are not in touch with any of their waves
I am holding Mine head by means of Bomb
Stops.

3.50 | R.18 / 3.50 | Very intense Bombardment of my
front line. All posts driven in by artillery
fire. Men accommodated in dugouts
Urgently require more men
Bombardment still intense especially
from Rossignol.
Lt Ryder severely wounded

R.19 | I have 55 men in all some of
whom are wounded. 2 Lewis guns only
two men to work them one of whom
wounded — Pans filled by Officers servant

R.20.
9.20 P.20 pm

I beg to report that at 9-20 P.M I saw 2
Germans removing our wounded back to their
lines from No Mans Land. As regards
numbers I have at present 56. Men
~~not today~~ including Stokes Mortars & H.C.
H.Z.R. I have also 1 officer 25 men 18th West
Yorks. Holding 3 posts in 9.3 area.
1 & 2 posts opposite Maxley Ave
Then there is a gap until you come to
Capt Furney who holds 4 posts inc. chett
S.f. Sap C. I have one post between
Sap C & Mark Copse
There are no Teams or M.G. in line
I am getting the wounded evacuated
as soon as possible but there are
a good number got to be attended
to
I have 5 Red Rockets at Sap C. & 12
Y. L. Lane Skies Rockets

WAR DIARY or INTELLIGENCE SUMMARY

Army Form C. 2118.

Place	Date	Hour	Summary of Events and Information	Remarks and references to Appendices
1/5 (S) Bn. EAST LANCASHIRE REGT	AUGUST 1916			
Locon	1-3		Battalion at La Locon employed on carrying parties to Trench Mortar Ammunition & construction of personal training.	
Trenches	4		Mons trip into the trenches along with the 125th Coy Lanc: Regt, & the Coy 125: York + Lanc: Regt, forming a Composite Battalion. Composite Battalion was found during trenches occupied by Oxford Regt & Kings Regt in the new CHAPELLE Sector.	
	5,6		Draft of 152 other ranks joined the Battalion, 68 infantry being 1 Coy 125: York + Lanc: & the remainder joined on August 7.	
	7/15		Reconnaissance of the 115: East Lanc: Regt. taking over from the line from Rouen to Kink St. supported by 1 Company 125: York + Lanc: Regt. Another Patrol consisted of 1/ officer & 21 men went in to attain an identification but was unsuccessful. Relieved by the 2/4 Leicesters and returned to billets in own of the battalion in Divisional Reserve. Casualties in the trenches 2 officers killed 2 wounded & OR killed 6 wounded.	
Locons	15			

Army Form C. 2118.

WAR DIARY
or
INTELLIGENCE SUMMARY.
(Erase heading not required.)

Place	Date	Hour	Summary of Events and Information	Remarks and references to Appendices
LEON	19		Draft of 3 Officers joined the battalion.	
	25		Working party of 2 Offrs & 100 OR. went to Merville	
	26		Battalion supplies working parties & is in Divisional Res. Pay and water were continued. General training	
CROIX BARBÉE	26.		Moved to Croix Barbé into Brigade Reserve.	
	30		Draft of 20 other ranks joined the battalion	
			1 Officer wounded	
	31.		Working party from Merville rejoined the battalion	
			Draft of 21 O.R. joined the battalion	

APers Lt Col.

Confidential

Vol M 7 59

7.Z.
3 sheets

War Diary.

11th East Lancs. R.   31st Division

September 1916

Army Form C. 2118.

WAR DIARY
or
INTELLIGENCE SUMMARY.
(Erase heading not required.)

Place	Date	Hour	Summary of Events and Information	Remarks and references to Appendices
11th Batt: East Lancashire Regt.	September 1916.			
Beaussart	2		Battalion took over a section of front line from 13th Batt: York & Lancaster Regt. Battalion H.Qrs. in RUE DU BOIS. Remainder of Batt: at Croix BARBEE. 9 Offrs. & Pvt.	
	5		Draft of 2 Officers, 77 Other Ranks. out 7 other ranks joined the battalion. 9 Offrs.	
	10		Battn Draft of 139 other ranks joined the battalion. 9Offrs. Battalion relieved by 12th Bn. West Yorks Regt. went into Army Reserve at VIEILLE CHAPELLE. 9Offrs.	
	11		Draft of 1 Officer joined the battalion. 9Offrs.	
	12		Battalion took over front line trenches on the right subsector of the FESTUBERT Sector from the 11th Bn Manchester Regt. (96 Brigade) 3 Companies held the front line and remainder in supports and 1 Company were attached to the 13th Bn. Manchester Regt. 1 Company in support in the Old British Line. 9Offrs.	

Place	Date	Hour	Summary of Events and Information	Remarks and references to Appendices
	22		Draft of Officers and 5 OR joins the battalion.	
	24		Relief was relieved by 13th Bahalion York + Lancaster Regt starting in the Village lines & FESTUBERT from the 4 13th York Lane Regt. Casualties while in the trenches 1 Officer and 1 ORs wounded & other ranks killed 1 wounded.	
	25		Draft of 1 Officer joins battalion. Billets at the Village were attacked. Patrols are of which was attached to the 13th York Lane Regt and one of which was attached to the 13th York Lane Regt. Both been in support in the R's Buildings.	
	29		The 2 companies in R's Buildings due to state Village num. on 29th Sept.	

E.C. Kirwin Hill.
Capt of R. Lancaster Regt.
1/11/16

Volume 8. 55

Confidential

11th Bn. East Lancs Regt.

War Diary.

31st Division

October 1916.

S.Z.
4 sheets

Army Form C. 2118.

WAR DIARY
or
INTELLIGENCE SUMMARY.
(Erase heading not required.)

Place	Date	Hour	Summary of Events and Information	Remarks and references to Appendices
11th Bn. Royal Lancaster Regt.	October 1916.			56
FESTUBERT	1.		Coy scouts dine Prive─ leant─ 13A braid from the 12th Bn. Unit Lancaster Regt. Battalion of 9.30 left Row on the night out. 12th Bn York Lancaster Regt on the left. Draft of 30 O.R. unslich battalion. O.R.	
	2.		Draft of 1 officer + 3 O.R.s came to Jones.	O.R.
	3.		Handed over line to 12th Bn. F.W. (?) support Regt and its was posted in VILLAGE LINE FESTUBERT from the 12th Bn. F.W. Kent Regt. Casualties while in trenches. 3 other ranks wounded O.R.	
VILLAGE LINE FESTUBERT				
	5.		Handed over VILLAGE LINE to 14th Bn. F.W. Kent Regt Lancaster Regt and marched to billets in LES CHOQUAUX.	O.R.
LES CHOQUAUX	6.		Marches from LES CHOQUAUX to ROBECQ.	O.R.
ROBECQ.			En route from Robec Cq to BERGUETTE where trains in entrained. Detrained at DOULLENS and marched to SARTON	O.R.
SARTON				

Army Form C. 2118.

57

WAR DIARY
or
INTELLIGENCE SUMMARY.
(Erase heading not required.)

Instructions regarding War Diaries and Intelligence Summaries are contained in F. S. Regs., Part II. and the Staff Manual respectively. Title pages will be prepared in manuscript.

Place	Date	Hour	Summary of Events and Information	Remarks and references to Appendices
SARTON	F-18		Battalion in billets at SARTON during the period, training carried out with a view to preparing the Battalion for an attack. One Brigade Scheme and one battalion scheme were carried out with cooperation of a Contact Patrol Aeroplane. On both occasions Hares and approaching the ground with attack were practised with success. Drafts amounting to 155 other ranks joined battalion during this period. ELR	
BARTNMONT WOOD 19	19		Battalion marched to camp in BARTNMONT WOOD. Training continued here and same time a tour of SARTON. Officers and N.C.O's reconnoitred the new line from HÉBUTERNE to CON IN CAMPS, especially the new communication Trenches from SW to the area, carrying parties for working parties in this area. forward "Dumps" etc. ELR	

WAR DIARY
INTELLIGENCE SUMMARY

Army Form C. 2118.

58

Place	Date	Hour	Summary of Events and Information	Remarks and references to Appendices
Ian dan	30 &		Relieved the 1st Batt: W. Yorks Regt in the trenches line taken over extending from JOHN COPSE (inclusive) to K.23.d.65.15 to HEARENBART JENA K.19.C.3.0. Also companies in front line and immediate support and two in reserve. Battalion on the left 1st R Scots Fusiliers. 1st R. York & Lanc. R	
	31.		Battalion on the right 1st R. Scots Fusiliers. 9th other ranks wounded SS. Canadian Bn 30/31	

R. Nivin. Lieut Colonel Cmdg
4/R. Lancaster Regt

Confidential

Volume XI—52

WD 9

War Diary.

11th Bn. East Lancs Regt

31st Division

November 1916.

9.Z
3 sheets

WAR DIARY
or
INTELLIGENCE SUMMARY
(Erase heading not required.)

Army Form C. 2118

53

Place	Date	Hour	Summary of Events and Information	Remarks and references to Appendices
11th Bn East Lancashire Regt				EUR
	March 1916			
Trenches DELL SAILLY au BOIS	1	—	Battalion in the trenches, holding the right sub-section HÉBUTERNE.	EUR
	3	—	Battalion relieved in the trenches by the 13th B. York Lancaster Regt and marched to DELL SAILLY-au-BOIS. Casualties in the trenches 1 killed, 2 wounded.	EUR
COIGNEUX to COURCELLES	7		Battalion left COIGNEUX. 2 Companies went to COURCELLES. 2 Companies went to temporary huts.	EUR
MARAIMONT to COURCELLES	10		Battalion instructed that 2 Companies at COIGNEUX must [illegible]	EUR
	11		3 MACHINE GUN DETACHMENTS were supplied by the Battalion to assist COIGNEUX for the purpose of assisting on	EUR
	12.		carrying parties on extrication wire & abatis of 1st Nov 13th	EUR
Trenches	14		Battalion moved into the trenches - taking over the right sub-section HÉBUTERNE from the 13th York Lancaster Regt -	EUR
			13th York Lancaster Regt to the left of the York Lancaster Regt	

Army Form C. 2118

WAR DIARY
or
INTELLIGENCE SUMMARY
(Erase heading not required.)

54

Place	Date	Hour	Summary of Events and Information	Remarks and references to Appendices
SAILLY au BOIS	15		In the left and 3rd Division on the right. Relieved in the line by 125 West Lancaster Regt. Casualties while in the trenches 6 killed, 14 wounded & 2 who died of wounds, Battalion to billets in Souastre a Bois.	EUR
Trenches	22		Lost Maj Cameron Keech this date from 125 West Lancashire Regt. Draft of [?] NCOs & men from 3rd Battn & officers [illegible] arrived	EUR
	25		Draft of 60 other ranks arrived	EUR
SAILLY au BOIS	25		Relieved by 125 West Lancashire Regt. Casualties from 22-25 4 killed & 11 wounded. Buses taken us to Sailly au Bois.	EUR
	30		Draft of 40 other ranks arrived. Battalion employed on emptying [?] parties & [?]	EUR

[signature]

Confidential

Volume 48

Vol 10

War Diary

11th Bn East Lancs Regt

31st Division

December 1916

Army Form C. 2118
49

WAR DIARY
or
INTELLIGENCE SUMMARY
(Erase heading not required.)

Place	Date	Hour	Summary of Events and Information	Remarks and references to Appendices
1st Battalion East Lancashire Regt No. 12. (December 1916).				
SAILLY- au-BOIS Trenches (HEBUTERNE)	1-2		The Battalion was in Brigade Support.	S/S
	3		Battalion relieved units trenches Nth of JENA trench from the 13th Battalion York and Lancaster Regiment. Frontage held from JOHN COPSE on the South to JENA trench on the North. She 3rd Division held the line to the South and the 12th Battalion Yorks and Lancaster Regt to the North. Major G.B. Armitage took over command of the Battalion vice Lieut-Col Figes.	S/S
			Draft of 3 Other ranks joined the Battalion.	
			Battalion was rested in the line by the 13th (S) Yorks and Lancaster Regt. Casualties for the period 3rd – 4th – 5 Other ranks wounded.	S/S
SAILLY-au-BOIS	4			S/S
	9		Two Enemies were attacks against the 4th (R) Unit Lancaster shaft in the joint trenches for Battalion.	S/S
Trenches HEBUTERNE	12		Draft of 14th Other ranks joined the Battalion.	S/S
	13		Battalion less two companies relieved two companies 14th (R) Bn Lancs	

WAR DIARY
or
INTELLIGENCE SUMMARY

Army Form C. 2118

Place	Date	Hour	Summary of Events and Information	Remarks and references to Appendices
POSSIGNEUL FARM (EQUIHEUX)			(continued) and Lancaster Regt in the front trench. June held by the battalion plus two companies 14th Bn. York and Lancaster Regiment. Right boundary K.23.a & 5.5.1. left Boundary Chortrivalricose. The 39th Division held the line on the right and the 93rd Brigade the line on the left.	6/15 6/15
	14		Draft of 5 other ranks joined the battalion. Battalion relieved by 12th Bn York & Lancaster Regt plus two companies 14th York & Lancaster Regt, 13th York & Lancaster Regt plus 2 companies 14th York and Lancaster Regt. 3 other ranks wounded.	6/15
	15.		Draft of 5 other ranks joined the battalion.	6/15
	23.		Draft of 16 other ranks joined the battalion.	6/15
	24.		Draft of 6 other ranks joined the battalion.	6/15
	25		Return for POSSIGNEUL FARM except devoted to training.	6/15
SAILLY-au-BOIS	25		Battalion less 2 companies moved to with Brigade Support at SAILLY-au-BOIS. Two companies attached to the 14th York Lancaster Regt in reserve line.	6/15
Trénelon (HEBUTERNE)	29		Battalion less 2 companies moved into the line. Battalion plus 2	6/15

Army Form C. 2118

WAR DIARY
or
INTELLIGENCE SUMMARY
(Erase heading not required.)

Place	Date	Hour	Summary of Events and Information	Remarks and references to Appendices
			Companies 14: York & Lancaster Regt held the line as from the 13th to 19th inst.	
			Casualties 29 O.R.s to gas inst. 4 Other ranks wounded, 4 other ranks killed.	
			Battalion on the right. 10th Gordon Highlanders	
			Battalion on the left. 11/5 Bn. East Yorkshire Regt.	

E. Bradshaw
Lieut-Colonel Commanding
14th Bn. East Lancashire Regt.

Confidential.

Volume III.

Vol XI

War Diary.

11th Bn East Lancs Regt. 31st Division

January 1917.

Army Form C. 2118   46

WAR DIARY or INTELLIGENCE SUMMARY
(Erase heading not required.)

Place	Date	Hour	Summary of Events and Information	Remarks and references to Appendices
			1st East Lancashire Reg't	
			Month XII N°II January 1917.	
Trenches. HEBUTERNE SECTOR	2.		Battalion plus 2 companies 14th B'n York/Lancaster Reg't in reserve in the front line trenches by 12th B'n York/Lancaster Reg't plus 2 companies	G/S
SAILLY-au-BOIS			1st B'n York/Lancaster Reg't. The whole battalion went into Brigade support at the DELL, SAILLY-au-BOIS, providing working parties for the brigade. Draft of 60 o/r ranks (First line battalion)	G/S
	5.		9th battalion moved to BEAUVAL après —	
BEAUVAL	11.		over to 9th B'n Cheshire Regiment. M/O's (?) were (?) broad to use the battalion. During the period at BEAUVAL the battalion has carried out indoors to Mustard, Rifle reading, musketry all ranks practices, CSM order Drill, specialist training, Physical training and Bayonet fighting. N.C.Os were used to assist in instruction. Companies were employed, on various mornings in the (?)	G/S

Army Form C. 2118

47

WAR DIARY
or
INTELLIGENCE SUMMARY

(Erase heading not required.)

Instructions regarding War Diaries and Intelligence Summaries are contained in F. S. Regs., Part II. and the Staff Manual respectively. Title Pages will be prepared in manuscript.

Place	Date	Hour	Summary of Events and Information	Remarks and references to Appendices
BEAUVAL	13. Jan		Draft of 3 officers joined the battalion.	S/S
	13.		Draft of 3 officers joined the battalion.	S/S
	19		The Army Commander inspected the battalion whilst carrying out training.	
			During the period at BEAUVAL, 15 other ranks joined the battalion on draft.	S/S
FIENVILLERS	22.		Battalion proceeded by march route to FIENVILLERS. Training at FIENVILLERS included the following:- Musketry practice on range, Platoon and Company in attack, Lewis Gun and Bombing instruction. Recreation during the afternoon.	
			On Jan 25th ——— January, the battalion paraded on lorry for parade and was inspected by the Brigadier.	S/S
			Draft of 50 other ranks joined the battalion.	S/S
FIEFFES	29.		Battalion proceeded by march route to FIEFFES, training continues to be at FIENVILLERS.	

Edward [signature]
Lieut Colonel Comdg.
11th Bn. Lancashire Fus.

1875 Wt. W593/826 1,000,000 4/15 J.B.C. & A. A.D.S.S./Forms/C. 2118.

Confidential

Volume XIV. 42

No 12

War Diary.

11th Battalion East Lancs. Regt. 31st Division

February 1917.

12.Z.
3 sheets

Army Form C. 2118

WAR DIARY
or
INTELLIGENCE SUMMARY
(Erase heading not required.)

Place	Date	Hour	Summary of Events and Information	Remarks and references to Appendices
	15.		Battalion East /an entire Regt. Manu XIV No II February 1917	
FIEFFES	15-19		Training was continued at FIEFFES and included Battalion and Brigade in attack on trench system. Spent in training in Open Warfare, including Advance to Contact, attack, Village fighting, attack.	LJR PJR PJR
TERRAMESNIL	20		Battalion proceeded by march route to TERRAMESNIL.	
COIGNEUX	21.		Preceded by march route to COIGNEUX and COIN. Headquarters and 3 companies being billeted in COIGNEUX and one company in COIN. Capt W.Lewis M.C. assumes temporary command vice Col.Mahon on leave.	PJR
	26		40 men detached to working party in the Back Area (BEAUVOIR Bns DÉPÉCHAMP, DOULLENS, MONTRELET + AUTHEULE).	LJR
	4.		The following drafts joined the Battalion during the month. 40 Base recruits.	PJR

Army Form C.2118

WAR DIARY
or
INTELLIGENCE SUMMARY
(Erase heading not required.)

Instructions regarding War Diaries and Intelligence Summaries are contained in F.S. Regs., Part II. and the Staff Manual respectively. Title Pages will be prepared in manuscript.

Place	Date	Hour	Summary of Events and Information	Remarks and references to Appendices
	9		29 Other ranks to B.E.F.	
	15		10 other ranks to B.E.F.	L.H.L
	25		2/Lt Lt LAUDERDALE a/S 2/Lt other rank to B.E.F.	L.H.L
	26		2/Lt LS.G. LONSDALE and 2/Lt T.E. CROWSHAW.	

L.H.Lewis Captain Commanding
11. R Lanc R.

2/3/17.

13.Z.
5 sheets.

Confidential

Volume XV

Vol 13

War Diary.

11th Bn. East Lancs Regt. 31st Division

March 1917

Army Form C. 2118
38

WAR DIARY
or
INTELLIGENCE SUMMARY
(Erase heading not required.)

Battalion East Lancashire Regiment
Vol IV No 3. March 1917.

Place	Date	Hour	Summary of Events and Information	Remarks and references to Appendices
COIGNEUX	1.		Battalion proceeded from Bertrancourt to THIEVRES by march route. Transport and QM details marching to AUTHIE.	S/S
	2.		Battalion preceded by march route to SAILLY DELL, less Transport returning to COIGNEUX.	S/S
	3.		Detached working parties supplied nightly for trenches. Nos 1 & 2 Coys. trenches. Coy from 2nd Gordon Highlanders. Line held ran length L 21 c and d. East of PUISIEUX. Line held was 2 lines of isolated posts with outposts and reserve in ORCHARD and GUDGEON Trenches and at the WUNDT WERK. Battalion HQr at WUNDT WERK. Line was held on left by 14th Bn. York & Lancaster Regt. and on the right by 2/4 Bn. York & Lancaster Regt.	S/S
	4.		On the night of 4/5, a party of 20 other ranks under 2/Lt WILD went out to examine a suspected enemy machine gun	S/S

WAR DIARY
or
INTELLIGENCE SUMMARY
(Erase heading not required.)

Army Form C. 2118

39

Place	Date	Hour	Summary of Events and Information	Remarks and references to Appendices
	9		men for covering and ascertain whether the enemy was holding Bucquoy Trench in strength. 2/Lt F.T.WILD and 3 other ranks are missing. — Lt. Col G.B. WHHOPE returns from leave. Capt F.K. DODSON and 2/Lt BATTERSBY and CROWTHER joined. Battalion headquarters moved from the WUNDT WERK to the Brickfields PUISIEUX.	S/S
	10.		Battalion relieved by 13th Batt York and Lancaster Regt and proceeded to billets in COURCELLES.	S/S
	11.		"A" Company returned to position as close to battalion headquarters as the 13th York Lancaster Regt and came under orders of O.C. 13th York Lancaster Regt for tactical purposes.	S/S
	13–16		1st. Company rejoined the battalion at COURCELLES. Remaining 3 companies employed on working parties. Battalion employed on working parties, constructing a railway to near SERRE.	S/S S/S

1875 Wt. W593/826 1,000,000 4/15 J.B.C. & A. A.D.S.S./Forms/C. 2118.

Army Form C. 2118
40

WAR DIARY
or
INTELLIGENCE SUMMARY
(Erase heading not required.)

Instructions regarding War Diaries and Intelligence Summaries are contained in F. S. Regs., Part II. and the Staff Manual respectively. Title Pages will be prepared in manuscript.

Place	Date	Hour	Summary of Events and Information	Remarks and references to Appendices
	15—25.		Battalion used its first hours free by march route, billeting at the places below on dates shewn.	EHS
	17.		AUTHIE	
	19.		BEAUVAL	
	20.		LIGNY (Jan 2 Corp at BETHUNE)	EHS
	21.		HERNICOURT	
	22.		FIEFS. (23rd inst was a rest day).	
	24.		ECQUEDECQUES (Jan 2 Corp for RESSES).	
MERVILLE	25—		MERVILLE (South side Canal)	EHS
	31.		Battalion training in musketry, Musketry, Bombing, Bayonet fighting. Specialists training.	EHS
			Casualties (other ranks) during March 1919. 4 killed, 15 wounded, 3 missing.	EHS
			Drafts	
	2.		12 other ranks.	
	16.		9 other ranks.	
	23.		10 other ranks.	EHS

Army Form C. 2118

WAR DIARY
or
INTELLIGENCE SUMMARY
(Erase heading not required.)

41

Place	Date	Hour	Summary of Events and Information	Remarks and references to Appendices
MERVILLE	26		2/Lt H. LINDER and E. HARRISON	&c.
	27		Capt J.S. LYLLIE, Lieut R. BATHURST, 2/Lt ENGLEACH, A/C. LETT,	&c.
			T.R. EDMONDSON, A.E. WOMERSLEY	&c.
	31		Capt S. WILLIAMS, 11th East Yorkshire Regt, attached.	
			In the field	
			1/4/19 M.	

Edwards
Lieut Colonel Cmdg.
11 E. Yorks R.

Confidential

Volume XVI
Vol 14

War Diary

11th Bn. East Lancs Regt. 31st Division

April 1917

L.B. 14.Z.
3 sheet

34

Army Form C. 2118
35

WAR DIARY
or
INTELLIGENCE SUMMARY
(Erase heading not required.)

Place	Date	Hour	Summary of Events and Information	Remarks and references to Appendices
			15th Bn. Royal Lancashire Regt. Nunc II No 4. April 1917.	
March	1-7		Battalion training - Reconnoitred work to support line between NEUVE CHAPELLE and FESTUBERT.	EHJ
FOUQUEREUIL	8-11		Proceeded by march route to FOUQUEREUIL on the 7th April. 4 Officers and 50 other ranks went to 170th SE Coy to the VIII Corps Reinforcement Camp at Thiennes where they were detached from parent to be behind since the battalion took part in any operations.	EHJ
HOUCHIN MAGNICOURT-EN-COMTÉ	action March 11 March 15		to HOUCHIN to MAGNICOURT-EN-COMTÉ on 14th April. Training continued during the period spent at MAGNICOURT. Specialist training and attack practice by platoons, companies and battalion.	EHJ
ECOIVRES	29		March to ÉCOIVRES	EHJ

Place	Date	Hour	Summary of Events and Information	Remarks and references to Appendices
MARŒUIL	Mar 30		March 5 to MARŒUIL to 30- April	
			Capt S. Williams 11= East Yorkshire Regt was attached to the	S/S
			Battalion on 15= April	
			The following drafts joined to the dates shown	
			7= April 9 Other Ranks	
			13= April 37 " "	
			21= April 6 " Recruits	
			29= April 4 " Recruits	S/S

Edward Ker
Lieut-Colonel, Commdg.
11= R. Lancashire Regt

Confidential

Volume XVII

War Diary

11th Bn East Lancs. R.

31st Division

May 1917.

Army Form C. 2118

WAR DIARY
or
INTELLIGENCE SUMMARY
(Erase heading not required.)

Instructions regarding War Diaries and Intelligence Summaries are contained in F. S. Regs., Part II. and the Staff Manual respectively. Title Pages will be prepared in manuscript.

Place	Date	Hour	Summary of Events and Information	Remarks and references to Appendices
			11th Bn. Royal American Regt.	
			Vol II H.Q.S. May 1917.	
Marœuil	May 1917 1.		Battalion marched from Marœuil to position East of Rœclincourt, preparatory to approach G6a. (Places keep France Shed 51 B.N.W. 1/20,000) coming under orders of G.O.C. 92nd Infantry Brigade. Battalion prepared to support 92nd Inf.Bde. on attack on oppr. Ross to position B21-b. (Sheet 51C M.W. 1/20,000)	S/d
Rœclincourt	2.			S/d
Front line oppr. Oppy	3.		Front line group line trenches from JC3 branch trenches to G22 by Battn. Frontage from B26 a & 4.1. G B12 c 6.5. Subaltern held wire & company in part line, one to support in B14 e rd and one in reserve West of Bailleul.	S/d
Bailleul	4.		Relieved by 13th E. York Regt and drew up position in reserve Catacombs B29a and B23c.	S/d
Bois in Q Maison Blanche	5.		Moved to trenches in Hic. temporary outpost/supporting battalion to right Infantry Brigade. Shot on heavy Gavrelle	S/d

1875 Wt. W593/826 1,000,000 4/15 J.B.C. & A. A.D.S.S./Forms/C. 2118.

Army Form C. 2118

31

WAR DIARY
or
INTELLIGENCE SUMMARY
(Erase heading not required.)

Instructions regarding War Diaries and Intelligence Summaries are contained in F. S. Regs., Part II. and the Staff Manual respectively. Title Pages will be prepared in manuscript.

Place	Date	Hour	Summary of Events and Information	Remarks and references to Appendices
Front line OPPY	9		Toit was OPPY. Subjected to H.E. & East Yorks Regt.	SBS
	9		Relieved by 13th Bn. Ymr (Lancaster Regt) early, with was supported Railway Cutting (B29a and B21c). Casualties up to May 9th: Killed, 2nd Lieut. T.W. James. detonprobe Munsiu and 3 Other Ranks. ———— Wounded. Capt. F. Williams, 11th E. Yorks Regt. and Lt. P. Ja. T. R., 2/ MPC left and 24 Other Ranks.	SBS
Railway Cutting BAILLEUL	10		Dept Hq 9 Other Ranks found the battalion 2/ LR Bendall and 9 Other Ranks wounded. 3 OR. killed. Stood to as ready to turn out on hostile attack was anticipated on from OPPY — Gavrelle.	SBS
Front line	12		Toit new OPPY. Subjected from 13th Ymr (Lancaster Regt). Enemy attempted a raid on Coy. 14.5 Ymr (Lancaster Regt) on the right. (Rifles were S.O.S. Nowthoson) with a party of support on trenches at B19 d.8. but were driven back by rifle and Lewis Gun fire.	SBS
	13th		Burying party under 2/Lt J.C. Lott. worked onwards up OPPY Trench will be	SBS

Army Form C. 2118
32

WAR DIARY
or
INTELLIGENCE SUMMARY
(Erase heading not required.)

Instructions regarding War Diaries and Intelligence Summaries are contained in F. S. Regs., Part II. and the Staff Manual respectively. Title Pages will be prepared in manuscript.

Place	Date	Hour	Summary of Events and Information	Remarks and references to Appendices
	4/5	1 am	Block N jothy the trench junction at B15 d.4.4 (Rifle Rifle Railway Copse ¾900). The objective was captured. Bombing attack made up OPPY Tr. under 2/Lt LOTT and bomb to under 2/Lt McKENZIE with the object of destroying two trench running from B15 d 67.20 to B15 d 44 Much of both parties were shot down by Mchn gun fire. Myster Enemy attempts to counter attack but were held up. 2/Lt LEACH and 2/Lt HUSINGER and 6 OR were killed and 5 OR wounded. 1 OR missing.	Ells
	11/9	3ᵃ	Attempt to bomb up OPPY Tr to B15 d 44 was made by Mr LOTT and a bombing party, but with out success, as the enemy were able to strafe any advance and several counter attacks were in progress.	Ells
			Relieved by 12 Bn. York & Lancashire Regt and returned to RAILWAY CUTTING. Casualties during 4 days tour in front line Officers and 7 OR killed and 36 OR wounded. Strength 18R.	Ells
	19/20		On the night 19/20 May the battalion occupied the RED Line in	Ells

WAR DIARY
or
INTELLIGENCE SUMMARY
(Erase heading not required.)

Army Form C. 2118

33

Place	Date	Hour	Summary of Events and Information	Remarks and references to Appendices
	20.		Bn. and B22 from employments details to realities for any enemy attack.	E/5
	26-27		Relieved by 4th Bedford Regt. in the evening and spent the camp at MONT ST ELOY	E/5
			Training at MONT ST ELOY. The Divisional Commander inspected training on 23rd May.	E/5
	27-31		Moved to camp at G46 3⁷ to combine with GREEN LINE	E/5
			Camping parties of 300 strong provided each night for work in H3d.	E/5
	31st		Drafts arrived on 13th, 14th & 19th May totaling 15 O.R.	
			Lt Col A.W. Rickman D.S.O took over command of the Battalion.	

Edward Holy Lt.
Cmdg. 11th East Lancashire Regt.

Confidential

Volume XVIII
VB 16 94/31

E.M. 16.Z.
5 sheets

War Diary.

11th Bn East Lancs. Regt   31st Division

June 1917.

Army Form C. 2118

25

WAR DIARY
or
INTELLIGENCE SUMMARY
(Erase heading not required.)

Instructions regarding War Diaries and Intelligence Summaries are contained in F. S. Regs., Part II. and the Staff Manual respectively. Title Pages will be prepared in manuscript.

Place	Date	Hour	Summary of Events and Information	Remarks and references to Appendices
	June 1917		11th Battalion East Lancashire Regiment Vol I No. 6. June 1917.	
ROCLINCOURT	1-9		Battalion continued providing working parties for work on the GREEN line and communication trenches. Casualties up to 9th June - 2 Lieut Hogan R.W.I and one other ranks wounded.	ans.
	10		Took over OPPY subsection from the Hawke Battalion, 63rd R.N. Division 22nd Bn. Royal Fusiliers on the left, 1st Bn. York's Lancaster Regiment on the right.	ans.
	14/15		Relieved by 13th Bn. York & Lancaster Regt. moving into Railway Cutting and trenches East of Bailleul. (2 Coy on Hill 50, Y Coy at Left Bn. H.Q.) and moving into Railway Cutting. Total casualties during tour of duty in line:- Captain E. H. Lewis and 8 other ranks wounded, 1 o.r. killed. During the absence of Lt Col Rickman, who was attending First Army Conference from 10th June to 19th June, the Battalion was commanded by Major J. E. Kershaw. Casualties from 18th to 19th:- 1 o.r wounded.	ans. ans. ans.
	19		Relieved in Railway Cutting by 11th Bn. East Yorkshire Regt. and proceeded to camp on Lens-Arras Road, near ECURIE. (G.4.a.2.P)	ans.

2nd Lt Hanfield H.B.

Army Form C. 2118

WAR DIARY
or
INTELLIGENCE SUMMARY
(Erase heading not required.)

26

Place	Date	Hour	Summary of Events and Information	Remarks and references to Appendices
	~~[scribbled]~~ 19—26		The Battalion was organizing and practicing for attack on CADORNA TRENCH, preparing the assembly positions and carrying up ammunition, water, stores etc. Casualties:— 1 o.r. wounded	—
	26/27		On the night 26/27th June, the Battalion took over the frontage allotted to it for the attack, from B.24.d.6.3 to B.24.b.66.70. This was held by one Company in the front line (RAILWAY TRENCH) one Company in MARINE TRENCH and two Companies in EAST BAILLEUL POST. Battalion Headquarters being at Battle Headquarters - B.24.d.15.86.	—
	27/28		The Battalion moved up into its assembly positions — three assaulting companies in the front line and the support company was accommodated in BLUE TRENCH. 'B' Company, 13th Bn East Yorkshire Regt. was the carrying company attached and joined Battalion on this night. It was accommodated in the old trench running from B.24.b.35.05" to B.24.b.60.35.	—
	28	7.10pm	The Battalion attacked with the 12th York & Lancaster Regt. attacking on the right and the 13th York & Lancaster Regt. attacking on the left. The Battalion objective was CADORNA TRENCH and WOOD ALLEY from head C.19.a.25.35 (exclusive) to GAVRELLE — OPPY ROAD at B.24.b.80.63 (exclusive)	—

Army Form C. 2118

 27

WAR DIARY
or
INTELLIGENCE SUMMARY
(Erase heading not required.)

Place	Date	Hour	Summary of Events and Information	Remarks and references to Appendices
			Company frontages were:-	
			Right Assaulting Company - Z Coy C.19.a.25.35 — C.19.a.12.58.	
			Centre Assaulting Company - X Coy C.19.a.12.58 — Tr. junction B24.b.96.70 (incl)	aux
			Left Assaulting Company - W Coy Tr. junction B24.b.96.70 (inclusive) — road B.24.b.60.83 (exclusive)	
			The whole of the objective was gained, the chief resistance being met on the left flank. The number of German dead actually counted in Battalion Area was 471.	aux
			Lt. Col. Rickman, having been selected by Brigade to remain behind with reinforcements left Battn H.Q. about midday and returned about 2.0 A.M. 29th June. During his absence Major J.O. Kershaw commanded the Battalion.	aux
			After dark one platoon from each of the assaulting companies was withdrawn from the objective to RAILWAY TRENCH in order to thin out the line	aux
30/1			On the night 30 June/1st July the Battalion took over the frontage previously occupied by the 12th York's Lancs and 13th York's Lancs extending from C.19.a.5.0 to B.18.d.72.00. The line was held with three Companies in the front line, one company in support in Railway Trench.	aux

WAR DIARY
or
INTELLIGENCE SUMMARY

Army Form C. 2118

Place	Date	Hour	Summary of Events and Information	Remarks and references to Appendices
			Casualties during period in line :-	
			27.6.17. Lieut. H. Welton and 25 o.r. wounded, 2 o.r. killed	Apx.
			28.6.17. (Day of attack) 2nd Lieuts Wheldon T.L. and Lonsdale W.F. and 40 o.r. wounded, 8 o.r. killed.	Apx.
			29.6.17. 17 o.r. wounded	Apx.
			30.6.17. 2nd Lieut Jackson and 10 o.r. wounded, 1 o.r. killed	Apx.
			Drafts arrived on 3rd, 11th, 14th, 18th and 23rd, totalling 30 o.r.	Apx.
			2nd Lieut. H.E. Richardson joined the Battalion from England on 6/6/17.	Apx.
			2nd Lieut J.E. Grimshaw ⎫	
			2nd Lieut W. Smith ⎬ joined the Battalion from England on 25/6/17.	Apx.
			2nd Lieut J.T. James ⎭	

A.W. Pickers
Lt Col
11th East Lancashire Regt.

Confidential

Volume xix
Vol. 17

L.B 17.2
3 sheets

War Diary.

11th Bn East Lancashire Regt 31st Division

July 1917.

WAR DIARY
or
INTELLIGENCE SUMMARY

Army Form C. 2118

Place	Date	Hour	Summary of Events and Information	Remarks and references to Appendices
	July 1917		11th Battalion East Lancashire Regiment Vol II. No. 7. July 1917.	
	1st		The Battalion was relieved in the line by the 13th Bn. East Yorkshire Regt. and proceeded to camp on Lens - Arras Road, near Ecurie (G.4.a.2.0.)	JMK
	July 3		Proceeded by march route to MAROEUIL and battalion went into billets there.	JMK
	"		Moved into canvas camp.	JMK
	4 - 13		Training at Maroeuil. Companies reorganized, three Companies now being purely fighting companies, the fourth company consisting of Coy Headquarters, Lewis Gunners, Signallers and all employed personnel.	JMK
	13.		The Battalion moved into close support in Mc ACHEVILLE Section, taking over from the 13th Bn. Royal Highlanders (Canadian Corps).	JMK
	18 - 19.		On the night 18/19th July the Battalion relieved the 13th Bn. York & Lancaster Regt. in the L 2 sub-section of the line. 92nd Inf. Bde. on the left, 14th Bn. York & Lancaster Regt. on the right. Frontage held was from T.17.d.75.75. to T.24.t.40.85. It was held by 2 Companies in the line (Left front company & Coy - Right front company Z Coy) and 1 Company (W Coy) in support.	JMK

Army Form C. 2118

WAR DIARY
or
INTELLIGENCE SUMMARY
(Erase heading not required.)

23

Place	Date	Hour	Summary of Events and Information	Remarks and references to Appendices
	21/22		Battalion relieved in the line by 16th Bn. West Yorkshire Regt and proceeded to Reynoldes Staging area. Then proceeded to Fraser Camp Mont St Eloy (F&H.6.4.)	J.V.K.
	22-29		Training at Mont St Eloy.	J.V.K.
	29.		Relieved the 16th Bn West Yorkshire Regt in the line on night 29/30th. in L 2 sub-sector of the Acheville sector. 93rd Inf. Bde on the left, 14th Bn York & Lancaster Regt on the right. Same frontage held as on 19th. Z Coy was right front company, W Coy left front company and X Coy in support. Total casualties for month :— 2 o.r. killed 3 o.r. wounded 2nd Lt. G. M. Bendall rejoined. 1 o.r. wounded. Following drafts joined during the month :— 4th. 12. o.r. 6th. 80. o.r. 17th. 6 o.r. 18th. 2/Lieuts E. D. Kay, F. H. P. Hodges, R. Hood, S. L. Browne, H. M. Saunders 26th. 1 o.r. 30th. 2/Lieuts G. Hood, J. Taylor. Total: 7 officers 112 o.r.	J.V.K. J.V.K.

J. V. Krahmer Major
for Lieut-Colonel
Commanding

Confidential

Volume XX
Vol 18

18.Z
3 sheets

War Diary.

of

11th Bn. East Lancs Regt

31st Division

August 1917.

WAR DIARY
or
INTELLIGENCE SUMMARY

(Erase heading not required.)

Army Form C. 2118

Place	Date	Hour	Summary of Events and Information	Remarks and references to Appendices
From line ACHEVILLE SECTOR	Aug 1917		Battalion East/on entire Reference VII X N.E. August 1917	
	1-4		The Battalion remained in the front line until it was relieved by the 13th Bn York & Lancaster Regt. They did the tatter when in Brigade Reserve near THELUS.	JR. JR.
THELUS	5-10		The period was attempted in providing working parties to the higher 10/17 trenches. The Bn Y+L Regt were relieved in the front line by the same parties of the right. The 14th York Lancs Regt	JR.
	11th		were in the right and the 9th Bn to the left. On 15th higher 10/17 relieved by 16th West York Regt and shared with Divisional Reserve at FRONT G ELEN (Areas C+D).	JR.
MONT ST ELOY	16-24		This period spent in training etc.	JR.
From line after system	24-31		Relieved 166 NF D.L.I. + Byers Supp N.I VILLEROY. Period spent in work on front line system & trenches & CT. Relieved the 13th Bn York & Lancaster Regt in the Bn Relieved tour...	JR. JR. JR. JR.

WAR DIARY
INTELLIGENCE SUMMARY

Army Form C. 2118
20

Place	Date	Hour	Summary of Events and Information	Remarks and references to Appendices
(cont inued)			The same postures as previously.	
	23.		1st CR Australian Div. proceeded on leave. Major Rhodes taking the command.	JR
			Our total casualties (today) were 1 Off. killed and 4 OR wounded. 3 Offrs (Capt K. Trenan, Capt P.J. Tarrant, and 2/Lt Wilson) and 23 OR joined in drafts during the month.	JR

J.N. Rhodes
Major Commanding
1st Bn P. Lancashire Regt.

Sept 30th 1917
L.S.S.L.B.

Confidential

94/31

Volume XXI

Vol 19

War Diary.

11th Bn. East Lanc Regt

31st Division

September 1917

W.D. 19.2

Army Form C. 2118

No. 15

WAR DIARY
or
INTELLIGENCE SUMMARY
(Erase heading not required.)

Instructions regarding War Diaries and Intelligence Summaries are contained in F. S. Regs., Part II. and the Staff Manual respectively. Title Pages will be prepared in manuscript.

Place	Date	Hour	Summary of Events and Information	Remarks and references to Appendices
	Sept 1917		11th Bn. East Lancashire Regt.	
Front Line ACHEVILLE	3/17		Von H H.Q September 1917	
	4/15		Relieved in the front line by 13th Bn. York Lancaster Regt. moving into Brigade Reserve vic Bert 1410 and I Coy at THELUS CAVES and	
THELUS			2 companies at the Railway Embankment near VIMY Station. During night the enemy bombed VIMY and the embankment with Phosgene Gas Shells (Yellow Cross) causing casualties to Officers & men.	
			114 DSR.	
FOURIE	7-		Relieved by 116 Canadian Battalion, "Batn detraining" to BEST CAMP RECLINCOURT and ROBERTS CAMP EURIE. Battalion other formed	out
	9-		Moved to SPRINGVALE CAMP EURIE	and.
FARBUS	11-		Moved in Brigade "B" Supports to the BROWN LINE, East of FARBUS WOOD	—

1875 Wt. W593/826 1,000,000 4/15 J.B.C. & A. A.D.S.S./Forms/C. 2118.

WAR DIARY or INTELLIGENCE SUMMARY

Army Form C. 2118

Place	Date	Hour	Summary of Events and Information	Remarks and references to Appendices
FARBUS.	1/15		Provided working and carrying parties from BROWN LINE.	—
WILLERVAL	15		Moved into Brigade "A" Support East of WILLERVAL in RED LINE. Provided working and carrying parties.	—
	11/24		One company attached to 14. Bn. York Lancaster Regt in the front line forming Brigade reserve.	—
FRONT LINE, 2d. ACHEVILLE.			Took over the front line from 14" Bn York Lancs Regt. One company 13" Bn. York Lancs Regt. was attached. Two coys held TH&Q7 — Bois 53. — Three companies in front line, attached company in support.	—
			13" Bn. D.L.I. were on right and a Canadian Division on the left.	—
ECURIE	25-		Relieved by 13" Bn. York Lancaster Regt. and lying Brigade Reserve at SPRINGVALE CAMP ECURIE	—

WAR DIARY
INTELLIGENCE SUMMARY
(Erase heading not required.)

Army Form C. 2118

17

Place	Date	Hour	Summary of Events and Information	Remarks and references to Appendices
In the Field	22 Oct 1917		Casualties during the week of exercise & for conditions as higher 4/5th unit – wounded F.O.R. Drafts – 2/Lt F.B.S. GARDNER and 69 O.R. joined the battalion at Corps Reinforcement Camp.	are. are.

A.M. Rahman
Lieut / Capt Comdg
1/5 Bn. E. Lancashire Regt.

Volume 11

Vol 20

War Diary

11th Batt. East Lancs R. 31st Division

October 1917

Cambrai

207
3 sheets

WAR DIARY
or
INTELLIGENCE SUMMARY.

Place	Date	Hour	Summary of Events and Information	Remarks and references to Appendices
	Oct 1917		11th Batt East Lancashire Regt	
			Vol II No 10 October 1917.	
Springvale Camp	1st		Battalion located at Springvale Camp near ECURIE	appx
Brown Line	6th		Relieved the 14th Batt. Y. & L. Regt in Brigade "B" Support in Brown Line S. of Farbus Wood	appx
Red Line	13th		Relieved the 14th Batt Y. & L. Regt in Brigade A Support in Red Line E. of Willerval. One company attached as support company to the 14th Batt Y & L Regt holding front line.	
	16th		(Willerval and) the Battalion area heavily shelled with gas shells and H.E. 35.O.R gas casualties in this battalion. Enemy attempts to raid the front line about 5.0 a.m - SOS was sent up and the whole battalion stood to - no further action was taken.	appx
Front Line ACHVILLE	18th		Took over the front line from the 14th Batt Y & L Regt, one company of 12th Batt Y & L Regt was attached. Frontage A.P. T17d 9.7. - T 30 a 5.3. Three companies in the front line, attached company in support. 18th D.L.I. were on the right and the 4.5th Division on the left.	appx

Army Form C. 2118.

13

WAR DIARY
or
INTELLIGENCE SUMMARY.

(Erase heading not required.)

Instructions regarding War Diaries and Intelligence Summaries are contained in F. S. Regs., Part II. and the Staff Manual respectively. Title pages will be prepared in manuscript.

Place	Date	Hour	Summary of Events and Information	Remarks and references to Appendices
	Oct 1917		11th Batt East Lancashire Regt Vol II No 10 October 1917	
	24th		Relieved by 13th Batt York and Lancaster Regt, moving into Brigade Reserve at Springvale Camp, ECURIE.	Appx
	30th		Relieved the 14th Batt. York and Lancaster Regt in Brigade "B" Support in the Brown Line. Rendezvous over Springvale Camp to the 13th Batt York & Lancaster Regt. Casualties during the month, exclusive of gas casualties on the 16th K.(R.) 1 O.R. (Wounded) 11 O.R. Missing 1 O.R. Death The following officers have joined the Batt. 10-10-17 Major J.H. Lewis. M.C 13-10-17 2nd Lt E.H. Bone. 14-10-17 2nd Lt E.D. Dowhen and A.Q.C. Nunn } since transferred to Leicester Regt. 15-10-17 2nd Lt J.L. Chandler 24-10-17 2nd Lt B.A. Horsfall, Q. Anderson, H. Hitt. Total number of reinforcements during the month 14 O.R. In the Field 1 Nov 1917	Appx Appx Appx Appx

A. M. Blackburn
Lt. Col. Commanding
11th Batt East Lancashire Regt.

Confidential

Volume 7

Vol 21

21.Z.
4 sheet

War Diary.

11th Battn East Lanc. Regt. 31st Division

November 1917.

WAR DIARY
or
INTELLIGENCE SUMMARY.

Army Form 2118.

9

Instructions regarding War Diaries and Intelligence Summaries are contained in F. S. Regs., Part II. and the Staff Manual respectively. Title pages will be prepared in manuscript.

Place	Date	Hour	Summary of Events and Information	Remarks and references to Appendices
FRONT LINE OPPY SECTOR	21		Relieved 11th E. Yorks Rgt. in OPPY Sector (Right Coy Subsector ONE) carrying out reliefs of 9th Infantry Brigade. Through lines C19a 35.75 — B25 t 15.12. 92nd Brigade on Right and 93rd on Left.	JJK
			Relieved by 13th Bn. York & Lancaster Regt. working via Bayeul.	JJK
ECOIVRES	22		Route at Springvan Camp. Reinf. Training — Platoon and Company.	JJK
	23–30		Orders — Major J. W. Watson MC. assumed command on 25th inst. until Major W. Keale-Amos returns from leave.	JJK
			Casualties during month apart from those mentioned above killed 2 OR. Wounded 2 OR.	JJK
			Inc. R/O. Bloke 23rd Lt. W.P.Taylor, 2.P.E. Dean, 7.H. Donoghue, J.H. Greenhill and J. West joined the battalion during the month.	JJK

WAR DIARY or INTELLIGENCE SUMMARY

Army Form C. 2118.   8

Place	Date	Hour	Summary of Events and Information	Remarks and references to Appendices
	November 1917		Vimy XIII No 11 11th Bn E. Lancashire Regt.	
Bivouac just [north of] FAMEUX	1-5		Battalion in "B" Support holding working parties for most went in to 4am to 5am [?] "A" Support.	JGL
RED LINE	6		N° 5 & 6 Pls line W. of ARLEUX n [?] were forming "A" Support and provided working and carrying parties.	JGL
FRONT LINE ACHEVILLE	11		Relieved the 14th Bn H.L. Regt in the front line. 9/23 Durham [?] were on the Right and 4/8 D.L.I. on the Left. Coy frontages held as previously.	JGL
	12	1pm	Battalion HQ heavy shelled WE astpo [?] others received. 2 O.R. Killed Lieut G. McRICHMAN and 4 O.R. wounded	JGL
ECURIE	19		Relieved by 13th Bn. W. Regt moving into Repose Caves or Arleux Camp Ecurie	JGL
Bois de la MAISON BLANCHE	20		Moved to ROUNDHAY Camp Bois de la Maison Blanche forming reserve to 92nd Infantry Brigade and early under order to go to ELEU dit on Bois of SE.	JGL

Army Form C. 2118.

10

WAR DIARY
or
INTELLIGENCE SUMMARY.
(Erase heading not required.)

Instructions regarding War Diaries and Intelligence Summaries are contained in F. S. Regs., Part II. and the Staff Manual respectively. Title pages will be prepared in manuscript.

Place	Date	Hour	Summary of Events and Information	Remarks and references to Appendices
			ST. O.R. joined Bn. March 26 remained under training as XIIIth Corps Makeup Keep reinforcement Camp. Capt. M.E. Trim was on Instructors (6/4/17) staff 8th Lancashire Fus. Division.	

J.M. Husler
Major Commanding
1/5 Bn. E. Lancashire Regiment

In the Field
1/XII/17

Confidential

Volume

VM 22

E.O. 22.Z
Hahult

War Diary.

11th Battn. East Lanc. Regt.   31st Division

December 1917.

WAR DIARY or INTELLIGENCE SUMMARY

Army Form C. 2118.

Place	Date	Hour	Summary of Events and Information	Remarks and references to Appendices
	December 1917.		11th Battalion E. Lancashire Regt. Vol II N° 24	
ECURIE	1-3		Battalion in Springvale Camp ECURIE continued training.	W.R.
OPPY	3		Relieved the 13th Bn York & Lancaster Regt in the front line history	W.R.
	-7		BRADFORD, BARD and BEATTY posts. The frontage has now extended to [B.15.d.F.12.] the 92nd Inf. Bde were on our right and the 13th Bn York & Lancaster Regt on the left.	W.R.
ECURIES	7		Battalion relieved by the 13th Batt. London Regt. proceeded to ECURIES Battalion in Camp and huts. After relief by Major LD Line K.C. Troop was evacuated to 11th Bn. Battalion in Camp.	W.R.
	8			W.R.
	8-20		Period of Rest. The spent in training and refitting. Platoon and company training carried out and our battalion practice attack.	W.R.

Army Form C. 2118.

WAR DIARY
or
INTELLIGENCE SUMMARY.
(Erase heading not required.)

Instructions regarding War Diaries and Intelligence Summaries are contained in F. S. Regs., Part II. and the Staff Manual respectively. Title pages will be prepared in manuscript.

Place	Date	Hour	Summary of Events and Information	Remarks and references to Appendices
NEUVILLE ST VAAST	20.		Moved to CUBITT Camp NEUVILLE ST VAAST (At 9 a.m. entrd.) by march rout. Battalion came into Brigade reserve to 1/2 Sub sector ACHEVILLE. Relieving 19th Canadian Battalion.	W.R.
	21-24		Training continued at NEUVILLE ST VAAST. Parties sent to ROCLINCOURT to watch trench wire 'entanglement'.	W.R.
	25		Moved into support to 1/2 Subsector ACHEVILLE, having CANADA & NEW BRUNSWICK Tr. Battalion HQ in VANCOUVER Road.	W.R.
	26-30		Companies working on front line and support trenches and improving wire in front of RED LINE. Relieved in support by 14th York Lancaster Regt. moving into Brigade reserve in Bivouacs Camps, Parva.	W.R.
	31		On 4/11/17 Capt C.Hamilton was mortally wounded R.G.W. captured by a hostile raiding party. 5 O.R. were wounded. One of missing officers has since been reported as wounded & a missing 2/Lt R.P. Anderson	W.R.

A 5834 Wt. W4973/M687 750,000 8/16 D. D. & L. Ltd. Forms/C.2118/13.

WAR DIARY
or
INTELLIGENCE SUMMARY.
(Erase heading not required.)

Army Form C. 2118.

Place	Date	Hour	Summary of Events and Information	Remarks and references to Appendices
			2nd Lieut A Champion to Tank Corps. — 2/Lt N. Brown to RFC — Capt R.S. Green to 99th Inf Bn as Staff Capt. — 2/Lt J.E. Prendera to England sick The undermentioned Junior Officers are reported — 2/Lt Capt Platt, 2/Lt W Powers, 2/Lt S. Gardner, 2/Lt A. Rees, 2/Lt Hs. Emett 2/Lt Pt Nicholas, 2/Lt F.R. Armstrong, 2/Lt H.L. Ross, 2/Lt T. Glendon Battn Casualties during December — Nil. Reinforcements — Nil.	

W.S. Row
Lieut Colonel
W.E. [illegible]

In the Field
January 1st 1918.

94th Brigade
31st Division.

1/11th BATTALION

EAST LANCASHIRE REGIMENT

JANUARY 1 9 1 8

Army Form C. 2118.

WAR DIARY
OR
INTELLIGENCE SUMMARY.
(Erase heading not required.)

1st Bn East Lancs Regt

74

Hour. Date. Place.	Summary of Events and Information.	Remarks and references to Appendices
1918		
January		
LAURIE	Corps	
1 – 5	Battalion in SPRINGVALE CAMP. Continuing training – introducing schemes of recreational training by means of organised inter-platoon contests in Tug of War & BBB practice.	
HUDSON POST.		
6 – 12	Relieved the 13th Battalion York & Lancasters Regt in the front line – one Company 12" York & Lancaster Regt in Battalion support in BRANDON TRENCH – Three "fighting companies" in NOVA SCOTIA, TRIUMPH & TOTNES TRENCHES, from T.30.A.7.5. to T.24.a.2.6. 5th Canadian Infantry Battalion on Left Flank – 12th Bn East Yorks Regt on Right.	

WAR DIARY OR INTELLIGENCE SUMMARY.

(Erase heading not required.)

75

Hour. Date. Place.	Summary of Events and Information.	Remarks and references to Appendices
CUBITT CAMP (Neuville St Vaast) 12th – 18th	Battn has "Z" Company (remaining attached to 13th York & Lancaster Regt in RED LINE) relieved by 14th York & Lancaster Regt: plus one Company 13th York & Lancaster Regt. Moved to Brigade Support in Cubitt Camp. Later – Company relief of Companies attached to 13th York & Lancaster Regt: on 15th.	
Vancouver Rd. 18 – 24th	Battalion plus 1 Company 13th York & Lancs Regt. plus "X" Company (1st East Lancs Regt in close support (RED LINE). Heavy frost which "broke" on January 16th resulted in bad thaw conditions. Trenches being knee deep in many places on 17th & 18th. Work during Tour confined to hard cleaning and improvement scheme of revetting Commenced on 23rd.	

Army Form C. 2118.

WAR DIARY
OR
INTELLIGENCE SUMMARY.
(Erase heading not required.)

76

Hour. Date. Place.	Summary of Events and Information.	Remarks and references to Appendices.
ECURIE 24" – 30"	Battalion plus 1 Company 13" Yorks hires Regt. relieved by 14" Yorkshire Regt. plus 1 Company 12" Yorkshire Regt. and proceeded to Brigade Reserve in Springvale Camp. Fighting strength of Battalion absorbed by working parties. – 1 Companies working in New Bar HQ at B17 a 55. One platoon working on Old Bryan HQ at B20 a 3.7. One platoon supplying "Pushing Party" for RE Train nightly.	
HUDSON POST 30 – 31st	Battalion plus 1 Company 12" Yorkshires Regt. relieved 13" Yorkshires Regt. plus 1 Company 14" Yorkshires Regt. in the front line & L2 Subsector at Hudson Post	

WAR DIARY
OR
INTELLIGENCE SUMMARY.
(Erase heading not required.)

Army Form C. 2118.

77

Place.	Hour. Date.	Summary of Events and Information.	Remarks and references to Appendices
In the Field	30 – 3' Contd	The following officers joined the Bn on January 13th – Lt G.H.B STANSFIELD 2/Lt. M ODDY 2/Lt P.E POSWELL 2/Lt B HAWLEY on January 16th Lt. H WILTON Battalion Casualties during January 1918 Killed — wounded 5 O.R. 9 O.R. 40 O.R. (15 remaining at Corps. M + R Camp for training (Signed) WD LOWE Lt Col Commanding 11th E Lang R	
	Feby 17th 1918		

WAR DIARY
or
INTELLIGENCE SUMMARY.

Army Form C. 2118.

(Erase heading not required.)

Place	Date	Hour	Summary of Events and Information	Remarks and references to Appendices
	January 1918		11th. Battalion East Lancashire Regt. Vol II No. 25	
ÉCURIE	1-5		Battalion in Sponvele Camp continuing Training - introducing scheme of Recreational Training by means of organized inter-platoon contests in Tug-of-War and B.B.B. practice.	W.R.
HUDSON POST.	6-12		Relieved the 13th. Battn York and Lancaster Regt in the front line - one company 12th York and Lancaster Regt in Battn Support in BRANDON TRENCH - three 'Fighting' Companies in NOVA SCOTIA, TRIUMPH and TOTNES TRENCHES, from 7.30.a.-7.5.6 T.24.a.2.b. 59th Cann. Inf. Battn on left flank - 12th Battn East Yorks Regt on right.	W.R.
CUBITT CAMP (NEVILLE ST. WAAFS)	13-18		Battn - less 'Z' Company (remaining attached to 13th York and Lancaster Regt in RED LINE) relieved by 14th York and Lancaster Regt plus one company 13th York Lancaster Regt. moved to Brigade Support in Cubit Camp. Entire Company relief of Companies attached to 13th York and Lancaster Regt on 15th.	W.R.
VANCOUVER ROAD.	18-24		Battalion plus 1 Company 13th York and Lancaster Regt. relieved 13th York and Lancaster Regt plus 'X' Company, 11th E.Lan. in Avre Support (RED LINES)	W.R.

23. Z

Army Form C. 2118.

WAR DIARY
or
INTELLIGENCE SUMMARY.
(Erase heading not required.)

Place	Date	Hour	Summary of Events and Information	Remarks and references to Appendices
VANCOUVER ROAD (Contd)	15-24		Heavy frost which 'broke' on Jan 16th, resulted in bad 'Thaw Conditions' - Trenches falling knee-deep in many places on 17th & 18th. Work during time confined to Trench clearance & improvement - Scheme of revetting commenced on 23rd.	W.R.
ÉCURIE.	24-30		Battalion, plus one Company 13th York and Lancaster Regt. Relieved by 14th York and Lancaster Regt. plus one Company 12th York and Lancaster Regt. Proceed to Brigade Reserve in Springvale Camp. Nightly Strength of Battalion absorbed by 'Working parties' - 2 Companies working on New Brigade H.Q. at B.14.a.4.4. One Platoon working on old Brigade H.Q. at B.20.a.37. - On ration supplying 'Pushing Party' for R.E. Train nightly.	W.R.
HUDSON POST.	30-31st		Battalion plus one Company 12th York Lancaster Regt. Relieves 13th York and Lancaster Regt. plus one Company 14th York Lancaster Regt. in the Front Line of L 2 Intracks at Hudson Post.	W.R.
			The following Officers joined the Battalion on Jan 13th - LIEUT A.H.B. STANFIELD. 2nd LIEUT M. ODDY, 2nd LIEUT P.E. DOSWELL, 2nd LIEUT B. HAWLEY — on Jan 16th LIEUT H. WILTON	
			Battalion Casualties during Jan. 1918 Killed Wounded 5 O.R. 9 O.R.	
			Battalion Reinforcements as 40 O.R. (15 remained at base 1917 camps for training)	W.R.
In the Field Feb 1st 1918				W.R. Lt Col. Commanding 11th Sherwood

www.ingramcontent.com/pod-product-compliance
Lightning Source LLC
Chambersburg PA
CBHW081439160426
43193CB00013B/2327